Keep It Simple, Sarah

Powerful Words
& Inspiration
for Christian Teen Girls

Heather Pettey

Wiseman Publishers

MEMPHIS, TENNESSEE

Published by Wiseman Publishers.

Book Cover Design by Heather Pettey.

ISBN Hardback 979-8-218-04927-0

ISBN Paperback 979-8-218-04928-7

Library of Congress Cataloging - in -Publication Data

Library of Congress Control Number:
TXu 2-330-983

Printed in the United States of America

For the girl who needs to know that you matter.

Refuse to let fear keep you from
living out God's purpose for your life.
When you hold back, play small, and hide
behind closed doors, you're not serving
anyone. We need your gifts and talents.
We need for you to be brave enough to
share them in your home, community,
and with the world. I love and believe
in you.

Praise for *Keep It Simple, Sarah*

With humor, insight and frame-worthy
visuals, Heather gently reminds us that we
have the power to write our own story.
'Keep It Simple, Sarah' offers Christian teen
girls a space to dream, to grow and live a life
of intention and purpose.

Stephanie Pletka, Author Living Your Best
Life: Host of Motherhood Mindset Podcast

IF YOU LOVE THEM, TELL THEM.

Telling someone you love them makes
that person feel good as well as
yourself. We all enjoy
hearing we are loved and
appreciated.
Love... do it... say it... mean
it... show it... live it.

You will NOT be
liked by everyone,
and that's OK!

Save your money.

DON'T BUY THINGS
TO IMPRESS PEOPLE.

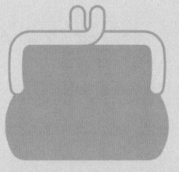

Individuals will be more excited
by your energy and willingness to serve
others than material things you own. A
kind heart and BIG smile will take you
farther than a new pair of fancy shoes.

Sleep

just right...

•8-10 hours

When exhausted, I'm...
played-out
fed up
annoyed
done-in
irritated
defeated
irked
bad-tempered
and occasionally nasty!

Treat HUMANS as well or better than your PET.

WHAT WILL THIS LOOK LIKE IN 20 YEARS?

Stretch, fade, tire of design

Stretch, leaves a scar

There are going to be times you'll
want to throw in the towel
and quit. Please don't. Nothing worthwhile
in life comes easy. Hard work
and determination will be a requirement
to be the person God created you to be.
Remember, if your dream was easy,
then it wouldn't be a dream.
There are few people willing to tromp
through the swamp,
climb over the mountains,
and wade through the water to
get to the good stuff. Be one of those people.
Believe in yourself.

"A winner is a dreamer who never gives up."

NELSON MANDELA

Keep Going

Quiet, silent moves get loud results.

It's so tempting, when you come in from
school, to just zone out in front of a screen. You're
exhausted from the challenges of the day,
teachers can be demanding, and being on your toes
around your peers all day can wear you out!

STOP SCROLLING & GO OUTSIDE.

Did you know spending time outdoors promotes
mental health? Nature lowers anxiety
and decreases stress. Being outdoors will also
make you feel happier overall. Challenge yourself
to at least 30 minutes a day.

I WILL

Life will seem hard sometimes.

NEVER

We all feel like we want to run away
when things get especially tough.

GIVE UP

When you are overwhelmed, stop and rest.

ON ME

Every situation looks better after a good night's sleep.

9

Get it out!

IT'S OK TO CRY.

Crying releases oxytocin and endorphins.
These "feel good" chemicals
are what make you feel better after a good cry.
So, don't hold back. Get it out,
and don't try to keep it all in.

Everyone cries sometimes.

Don't speak negatively about your boyfriend's family.

Be extremely careful when discussing your boyfriend's
family, and stay on the positive side of the fence.
Creating drama will be detrimental to your relationship
with everyone- especially your boyfriend. Shedding
bad light on your boyfriend's family sends a message that
you are immature and care much more about your own
feelings than his. You don't have to be BFFS with
his sister, but you do need to be polite.

LIMIT SUGAR.

*Scientists have linked a diet heavy in sugar, junk food, and fast foods to an increased risk of anxiety and depression.

Some make gossiping a hobby, and you want to beware of those people. If they talk about others to you, then they will speak about you to others too. They cannot be trusted. If your friend or acquaintance is dishing out someone's business, gently excuse yourself from the conversation. If this is not an option, then quickly change the subject.

Gossip

NO NO NO

Don't be a
spreader
of bad news.
Exodus 23:1

2 EMPATHY
SIDES REACHING OUT TO EACH OTHER,
OPENING UP TO TRY TO UNDERSTAND
THE OTHER'S FEELINGS.

I WILL NOT RISK MY LIFE.

I will not endanger my life and the life of others by TEXTING & DRIVING.

I am
FRee
to be myself!

WRAP

your arms around
those who are hurting.
Life can be hard sometimes.

·Forks = left of plate

·knives and spoons = right

·knife blade faces plate

·Stemware above and right of the dinner plate
·bread-and-butter plate to the left of place setting.

You have the power to change someone's
life with your words and facial expressions.
Use your abilities for good.
Never pass up a chance to build
someone up. It's a gift from you to that
person, and it's completely free.

Build people up!

Turn the corners of your mouth up
and smile! LIGHT UP THE ROOM!

IF YOU DON'T LIKE THE
ROAD YOU'RE WALKING,
START PAVING ANOTHER ONE.

Dolly Parton

just because your

Being told "no" by your parents or someone in charge of you
can be frustrating. You want to call your own shots,
make your own rules, and we sometimes become
angry when things don't go our way.

parents tell you "NO"

It's important, during these times, to
remember how much you are loved. Your caregiver only wants the
very BEST for you, and their job is to direct and help you
make good choices that will benefit future you.

doesn't mean they

A "no" takes much more effort than a yes.
Maybe, they are protecting your reputation, or see
things that you are unable to recognize. More times than not, a
"NO" means I LOVE YOU!

don't love you

Words can hurt.

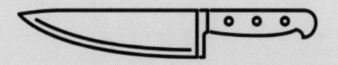

"The world needs strong women. Women who will lift and build others, who will love and be loved. Women who live bravely, both tender and fierce. Women of indomitable will."

Amy Tenney

Make sure the you
on the inside
matches the you
on the outside.

VAPING IS FOR LOSERS...
and you're not a loser.

"No matter what you look like or think you look like, you're SPECIAL, and loved, and perfect just the way you are."

Tyra Banks

The day you were born, everyone
gathered to see you and discuss how perfectly
you were made. You arrived full of potential... all shiny
and new. You were created for a reason that was known by your
heavenly Father long before you were born, and
He has positioned you to take advantage of opportunities,
as they are all around.

You are bursting with possibility.

YOU ARE GOLDEN

Psalm 139:13-14

TOP 4 TIME WASTERS

☐ SCROLLING SOCIAL MEDIA

☐ GOSSIPING

☐ TALKING TO YOUR EX BOYFRIEND

☐ WORRYING

8 reasons to *make your bed*

encourages organization
feeling of accomplishment
reduce stress
better productivity
sense of calm
improved focus
better sleep
improves mood

there's no
way to know
some things
until you
get there.

"If you are always trying to be normal, you will never know how amazing you can be."

— Maya Angelou

If your goal is to be like everyone else
and blend in with the crowd, then we will never
know the real you. The world will be deprived of
your uniqueness, and that would be just plain sad.
Besides, constantly trying to "fit in" with the
crowd is exhausting. Direct that energy towards sharing
your gifts, so we can all benefit from knowing
the authentic version
of YOU!

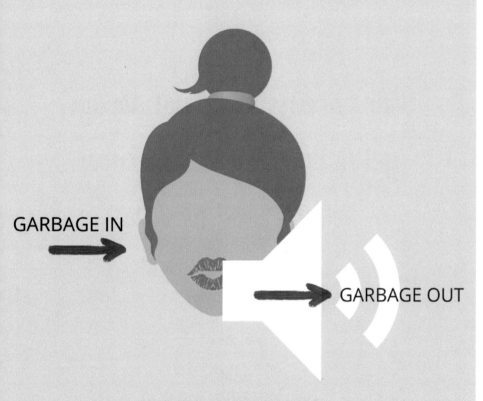

GARBAGE IN

GARBAGE OUT

Fill your heart and mind
with lovely words and ideas,
and they will come streaming
out of you like SUNSHINE
beaming through the clouds
on a hazy day.

Your parents might not always

Sure, you may consider your parents to be old fashioned,

get it, but they usually know

and maybe they are, but never discount an idea

what's good for you.

just because it's not your own.

Come out
and say hi
sometimes

How you
dress will
attract a
certain
kind
of guy.

Life doesn't always
go as planned.
Don't have just one.

NOBODY WILL EVER LOVE YOU LIKE YOUR

MAMA

BE GOOD TO HER.

She is clothed with strength & dignity, & she laughs without fear of the future.

take alcohol seriously

Approximate # of teens who die as a result of underage drinking every year

5K

Don't unfollow friends and family on social media when you get angry. It makes you look small and points out your lack of maturity.

*You're better than this!

**DON'T HOLD OTHERS
TO A HIGHER
STANDARD THAN
YOU HOLD YOURSELF.**

Change your 🪥

every **3** months

Focus on **1** thing at a time. You can't do "all the things" all the time.

If you can't be kind, don't be anything at all.

There are circumstances in life that are
out of your control. People will sometimes
be cruel and mean spirited. Recognize it
and step away. It has nothing to do with
you and everything to do with how they
think and feel about themselves.

Don't participate.

If you don't try,
my friend,
you can't win or learn.
You will just stay stuck,
and no one wants to
be stagnate.

the only way to fail

is to not even try

Try over
& over
& over
& over
& over
AGAIN!

I will not be pressured into having

SEX

Don't let anyone pressure you,
persuade you, or give
you an ultimatum.
It's not an, "If you don't do this,
then I won't do that."

Your BODY BELONGS TO YOU. YOU GET TO DECIDE.

If he loves you, then he will wait, and there is **NOTHING** wrong with waiting.

START HERE

You don't have to be great to start, but you have to start to be great.

Zig Ziglar

No more excuses! Today is the day.
How will tomorrow be better than today? What will
change? You don't need all the answers before you
start. Today is the perfect day to begin. You will
figure it out as you go. Don't wait another day.

I will surrender to the things that are out of my control.

There is much about life that
is out of your control.
What others think about you,
the way others choose to treat you.
The weather. The cost of milk.

Concentrate on things you can control...
YOURSELF!

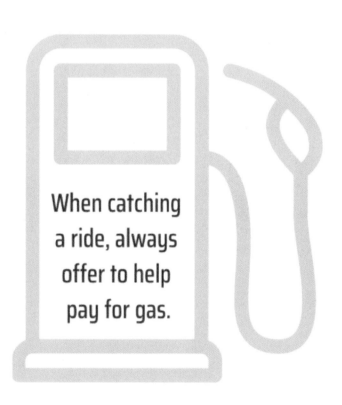

When catching
a ride, always
offer to help
pay for gas.

Sometimes "I love you," sounds like...

"Did you have fun?"
"What did you eat?"
"Who did you hang out with?"
"What did he say?"
"Do you want to go for a walk?"
"I'm praying for you."
"I thought about what you said."
"You look beautiful."
"I hope you feel better."
"I'm so proud of you."
"This reminded me of you."
"Be careful!"

When you unplug, you make room for real life!

Become so busy being passionate about
your own life, that you lose interest in watching
everyone else's play out in social media. Do more things
that LIGHT YOU UP and cause you to forget
about your phone. You still have best friends out
there to meet, people to serve, places to go,
new things to try. Life is happening now.
Challenge yourself to MORE doing and LESS observing.

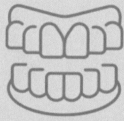

Always tell friends and family

if they have food stuck in their teeth.

We complain a lot of times of the things we have
to do, but what if we were unable? How would that feel?
What if we mentally or physically couldn't do the things we so
often dread doing? What would life look like if we couldn't
walk to clean our room or couldn't think well enough
to do our homework? Perspective is everything.

Instead of "I have to" say "I get to!"

Life is an opportunity and not an obligation.

Truly successful people do life
with a mindset of gratitude.
They recognize that everyday is a gift,
and they don't take their God-given
abilities for granted. They use them!

shower and get dressed
E V E R Y D A Y

ALWAYS LOOK YOUR BEST

YOU'LL NEVER GET A 2ND CHANCE
TO MAKE A 1ST IMPRESSION

YOU'LL LOOK BEAUTIFUL

"Come to me, all you who

are weary and burdened,

and I will give you rest."

Mathew 11:28

SHOW UP WHEN MOST PEOPLE GIVE UP.

Congratulations!

When good things
happen to your friends,
the words coming out
of your mouth should
sound like this...

Great
Job!

WOW!
You did it!

Always
celebrate
other's
wins.

I'm so
proud of
you!

Your hard work
paid off!

Stop dreaming.

Start doing.

A handwritten
thank you note &
thank you text are
not the same thing.
*Write the note.

Remember, the words
you say to yourself matter.

I DIDN'T DESERVE
THE MEAN THINGS
I SAID TO ME

Speak to yourself as you would your best friend.
You would never tell your best friend
she was a loser or call her unattractive.
You're on your own journey, and you have endless growth
potential. When you have a negative thought about yourself,
stop and replace it with a positive along with an example
or evidence of good. WRITE IT DOWN, and SPEAK it aloud.

Learn from your mistakes, but don't carry them around.

Don't harp on what you did or didn't do.
It will not change what has already happened.
And don't keep making the same mistakes over
and over again. Learn, grow, and improve.

If you are scared, tell someone.
If you are hurting, tell someone.
If you are sad, tell someone.
If you are worried, tell someone.

When life gets heavy, reach out.
Don't carry the load all by yourself.

"May your choices reflect your hopes not your fears."

-Nelson Mandela

Respect your elders.

Some of the best days of your life haven't even happened yet.

There is so much to look forward to,
and you can't even imagine all that God has
planned for your life! Stay faithful, and put God
first in EVERYTHING you do. Be sure to pause and
recognize the goodness in your life.

Y O U R

growth has nothing

to do with your growth

as a human being.

Sometimes you don't get what
you deserve, because you deserve
way
BETTER

WAY MAKER, MIRACLE WORKER, PROMISE KEEPER, LIGHT IN THE DARKNESS MY GOD THAT IS WHO YOU ARE

-Sinach

You can try replacing Him with people
and things, but they will never measure up.

I love you no matter what.

we begin and end with family

family is EVERYTHING

if you have family, you are wealthier than you think

don't be mean   love your people

Families are the compass that guides us. They are the inspiration to reach great heights, and our comfort when we occasionally falter.
Brad Henry

they believe in you

Home is people. Not a place.

forever...for always

EVERY MOMENT MATTERS

be good to the people who love you

**Making RUDE & HURTFUL
comments on social media
only makes you look RUDE & HURTFUL.**

IMPERFECT = PERFECT

PERFECT IS BORING, OVERRATED, AND DOESN'T EVEN EXIST.

NEWSFLASH!!! No matter how hard you try,
you will never be perfect. The celebrities and
influencers you follow are imperfect as well. Just
be the best version of you, and learn to be proud of
yourself. Know that your best is enough,
and in God's eyes, you are perfectly made.

NEVER BE THE...
ENVIOUS,
JEALOUS,
INSECURE STUFF
KINDA GIRL.

BE THE...
"I'M CHEERING FOR YOU!"
"I WANT THE BEST FOR YOU!"

KINDA WOMAN.

NEVER LOSE HOPE.

GOD SAW IT ALL,

AND HE HAS A PLAN.

His plan is PERFECT

Proverbs 3:5-6

The sooner you figure out
which chairs don't belong
at your table, the more
peaceful your meals become.

LIFE IS FRAGILE.

REMEMBER WHO YOU ARE AND WHO YOU BELONG TO, AND YOU WILL BE SET FREE.

ROMANS 14:7-9

When you
fall off,
get back on!
Don't make
excuses and
don't wait.
Up you go!

Be
Generous

with your kind words, so your ♥
will continuously spill
love.

MAKE HIM
BUY THE COW!

***The world will tell you it's a
good idea to live together before
marriage, but it's a total lie.**
The act of moving in before a wedding robs you
of the excitement of the honeymoon phase, and
you will completely short change yourself. Also,
studies show a higher rate in divorce of those
who live together prior to marriage.

JEALOUSY WORKS
THE OPPOSITE
OF THE WAY YOU
WANT IT TO.

Never let anyone separate you
from the ones you love.

Have you ever noticed
the people who are the
most fun to be around are
the ones who laugh a lot?

NEVER TAKE YOURSELF TOO SERIOUSLY!

Laughing at yourself not only
makes life more fun, but it also
shows that you are a humble
person. Acknowledging your
flaws is freeing. You will also be less
likely to get offended by other's comments.

IF YOU STUMBLE,
MAKE IT PART OF THE DANCE.

You're going to make
mistakes, and that's ok.

Everything is
FIGUROUTABLE
Marie Forleo

As long as everything is about you, everything can't be about

JESUS

DO THE SCARY THINGS!

YOU CAN'T ACHIEVE YOUR DREAMS
IF YOU ARE ALWAYS PLAYING IT SAFE.

DO MORE OF WHAT WORKS

kindness • nice manners • study hard • pray • save money• simplify
honesty • hard work • stay positive • encourage others • smile
empathy • believe • generosity • humble • trustworthy • loyal
genuine • grow • focus • gratitude • exercise • respect • LOVE

AND LESS OF WHAT DOESN'T.

1

THERE IS

ONLY

one true God, and I'm NOT Him. I'm not in control.

Always give a firm handshake
and look them in the

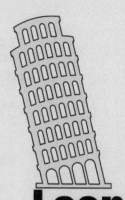

Lean in when someone is speaking and really listen.

Take time to get to know people.
There's so much we can learn from each other,
if we will just be quiet and listen.
God always puts people in our lives for a reason.
Some are sent to teach us a lesson and some
are meant to be a blessing. Not everyone
is expected to stay.

DRUGS WILL KILL YOU

STAY CONNECTED

with the
people you love ♡

Be willing to take trusted advice.

PROVERBS 12:15

A good HOUSEGUEST...

- Arrives with a small gift.

- Leaves pet at home unless invited.

- Makes bed and keeps room and bathroom tidy.

- Is always respectful of house rules.

- Has a pleasant attitude.

- Offers to help with meal prep.

- Asks what to do with linens and towels before leaving.

- Removes garbage.

- Sends a handwritten thank you note following the stay.

not so
F A S T !

I would rather be the Sally who was late, than the late Sally.

Everyone did whatever seemed right to her.

Judges 21:25

The world will tell you to do whatever makes you happy. YOLO. Make your own decisions based on what you know is right. You will make mistakes. Get knocked down. Get back up, and ask for forgiveness. No sin is greater than God's love for you.

DON'T SHOW EVERYONE YOUR BUSINESS.

Some things should stay private.

NEVER OVERSHARE.

"I CHOOSE MODESTY."

CALM THE DRAMA

DON'T ADD TO IT.

Kindness is contagious
but so is grumpy. Spread
kindness and don't get
involved in drama.

You know by now how it works, and it NEVER
turns out good. Your friends begin arguing,
then it's, "she said, she did," and no one wins.
Don't add to the issues. Rise above it.

Want to prove to your parents
that you're growing up?

Clean. The. Kitchen.

It feels good to be pampered and waited on,
but true joy is in serving others. Participating
in household jobs is an opportunity for you to prove your
level of maturity in recognizing the need to work together
as a family. Teamwork keeps your home functioning well. When you
pitch in and help without resentment, it says to
everyone, "I am growing up!"

Don't change
so people will
like you.
Be the real you,
& the right
people will
love you.

ACKNOWLEDGMENTS

To David, thank you for letting me pursue all of my dreams. As my husband and best friend, you love and encourage me through all my projects, and I'm so appreciative- I love you. To my children, Anna Blair, Carson, Reed, and Winston, you are my "why" and my greatest gifts. I love you more than you will ever know! Thank you to my mother, Sherry, you've taught me to pivot, follow my gut, and go after it. Thank you for being my loudest cheerleader- I love you so much. And in honor of my late step-father, Quentin, for always believing in me. Thanks to Joe and Judy for being the most wonderful in-laws! Your continuous love and support never goes unnoticed, and I love you both. A special thank you to my BFFS. You are my forever partners in crime, and I'm so thankful for your friendship and support. You know who you are, and I love you to pieces! In remembrance of my Memaw, your love is EVERYWHERE, and you are missed EVERYDAY. Thank you for sharing Jesus with me 24 hours a day 365 days a year. I'd also like to thank God, who continuously reminds me that I'm never alone, and we are all here for a purpose. He gives me all I need and more than I deserve. He sees all of my imperfections, and yet, He still loves me. I am forever grateful.

Heather is a perfectly imperfect wife to David. mom to 4 amazing humans. and lover of Jesus. She is passionate about encouraging moms to remain sane and find joy while parenting teens. The laughter and support happens weekly on her podcast. Life Coach BFF Show. When not podcasting or curating for CLUB BFF (a membership for Christian moms of teens). she's coaching moms to live confidently. set clear boundaries. and find their purpose while parenting. Heather is also a huge advocate for children in foster care and a supporter of adoption.

Originally from the Mississippi Delta with a BA in Communications from Mississippi State University. Heather has made appearances on CNN Headline News and other media. She believes that life is a long line of lessons. and in her opinion. it's all about faith and good ol' common sense. Heather happily resides with her family in Memphis, TN.

Heather@HeatherPettey.com

LIFECOACHBFF @lifecoachBFF

Made in the USA
Las Vegas, NV
05 December 2022

60052729R10067